W9-CSD-214

News from the World at My Birth:
A History

Peter Weltner

Standing Stone Books
Syracuse • Brussels

News From the World at My Birth: A History

Copyright © 2010 by Peter Weltner

First Printing

Standing Stone Books is a division of **Standing Stone Studios**, an organization dedicated to the promotion of the literary and visual arts.

Mailing addresses:
951 Comstock Avenue, Syracuse, New York 13210 U.S.A.
and
Jesserenstraat 58, 3850 Borgloon, Brussels, Belgium.

Email: info@standingstonestudios.org

web address: www.standingstonestudios.org

Standing Stone Books are available in both print and ebook formats.

Printed by Versa Press, Inc. 1465 Spring Bay Road,
East Peoria, Illinois, 61611.

ISBN: 978-0-979-1944-4-3

Library of Congress Control Number: 2010937184

Cover and text design by Adam Rozum

Standing Stone Books is a member of the Literary Council of Magazines and Presses.

News from the World at My Birth:
A History

Peter Weltner

For my sister, Diane Strommer

A Raven's Dance

Whether we are born there or not, whether we chose to leave it or not, the past is the country we all emigrate from. It leaves its mark on us, and we return to it, like immigrants to their lost homes, to find not only who we once were but who we still are. Yet it is also foreign to us, a mystery, living as we do in another world we call the present: "The past is an art of unseen wings that beat in the visible dark" ("The Birds").

The 'My' in the book's title is elusive. It renders particular the implicit 'our.' These poems are not autobiography. They tell stories taken from newsreels, histories, and movies of the period and from anecdotes the poet was told by those who were there. But like the son staring into his sick old father's eyes at the end of "Pilgrimage," the poet stares into the past's eyes as if secrets hide behind them, "like clues to the world at his birth no father ever tells his son." The past keeps secrets we long to know and to understand. It is our father, our mother. But it knows what is too dangerous to reveal to us plainly, the death-haunted world into which we are born. Its war-ravaged landscape is our own.

What stories do these poems tell? It is the time just before, during, and after the Second World War, some of its battles present in this book: Kasserine Pass in North Africa, Anzio, the Ardennes, Luzon in the Philippines, Peliliu, Saipan. Some fight in it, some wait for those who do. Some return from it, some do not. Some are children of survivors, some of the dead. But more of its stories take place stateside, in cities or in the country. A young nurse and a very old man together wait for news in a nursing home. Reading a picture book, a girl fantasizes about attending operas at the Metropolitan. Mob violence hits a big city. A mother mourns the drowning of her son by submarine warfare in the North Atlantic. A photographer takes pictures of his assistant dressed in his brother's uniform. A sailor's life is detoured by a murder during a three day leave in Manhattan. A priest tends his flock in a Brooklyn parish. Their father killed in Saipan, two brothers slowly close their house to the rest of the world. A soldier who has survived the war in the Pacific remembers his brother who was killed in it. Two elderly men–one a rich, reactionary aesthete, the other a member of the Communist Party who fought in Spain as well as later in France–momentarily stand side by side, like neighbors, as a destructive storm floods the peak of Telegraph Hill. In the midst of such violence, there is also sometimes communion, even love. Gifts are given, received, accepted. In the world's night, flowers may sometimes bloom. A soldier's love, thought gone for good, returns to him. An old soldier's son, after much mourning, begins his own pilgrimage, "the true face of God... beckoning him to more."

"Each person now alive mirrors someone who has died or is yet to be born." So, too, do "the dreams of dreamers long dead recur" in each of us. In the book's last poem, "The Birds," the past is like a raven's dance, their black wings invisible as they prance about at midnight. But still we stare into that dark because, like place, the past is who we are. Sixty five and more years ago the world fought a terrible war, one that continues in our souls, our hearts, our minds, even if we're not conscious of its presence. These poems speak of how real the past still is, how much it still pleads, "Give us peace." It is the essential prayer–none more holy, more sacred, the one memory teaches us to say, even sing more than any other. All the poems in this book pray it, however much, at times, they must do so silently, in what remains unspoken inside every story, unsounded in every poem's music. But poetry, in love with words, may be an art more keenly aware than any other of the need for silent prayer:

Say

he sleeps peacefully now, my son, unafraid,
lights off, behind a door I hated to close.

Linda Gregg, author of *All of It Singing: New and Selected Poems*

To Flower by Night

Peter Weltner's *News from the World at My Birth* is filled with characters and stories. Almost all take place just before, during and just after the Second World War. The book is, among other things, a great read, almost a page turner. This is extremely unusual in a book of poetry, but then, these are amazingly individual and unique poems. The voice is dense, articulate, highly educated (though the characters may not be), charged with erotic intensity and pain. There is much violence here, some of it shocking, yet there is discretion as well, which only deepens the impact on the reader. Some are written as prose pieces; others are in relatively short lines. What I love about them is that they lodge deeply, in the subconscious – you simply cannot get them out of your mind.

One of the best is "Three Day Leave", a 7 page narrative poem, whose protagonist, Curt, on leave, checks into a New York flophouse, wanders around the City, meets and beds another man, comes back dead drunk, and, after a hideous drunken brawl, wakes up to find his pocket knife embedded in another man's heart, goes AWOL, hops a train, steals a car, and continues west, picks up a boy who has just been drafted and is terrified, changes clothes with him, changes identities in essence, and the last we see of him is somewhere in the Philippines:

> Luzon. Each trail bend exposes more jungle.
> In the mountains, the thunder is manmade. Afraid,
> they hide in empty caves. His stools are bleached as bones.
> Though dizzy from disease, he sees the trigger wire
> concealed in an overgrown path to an old stone bridge
> and safely guides his men around it to a stream
> where flocks of birds flap their wings and squawk
>   like sullen gulls.

The lyricism is subtle. The language weaves its way through a rich landscape, whether the rural South, a seedy section of New York or Los Angeles, or a bombed-out ruin of a German village near the end of the War. The tone is invariably calm, even when what it portrays is not. It is a voice you can trust, even when it leads you into some of the darkest regions of the heart. There is something fundamentally religious in its sensibility. Not in an easy, comforting or dogmatic way, but in the sense of things mattering, and mattering deeply.

The opening poem "Bodysnatchers" (from the famous '50s Science Fiction film) sets the tone:

> *Dreams*
> *root in whoever sleeps dangerously long.*
> *Thereafter the world is not their home. To flower*
> *by day was nothing. To flower by night is song.*

This is a marvelous book. It demonstrates the necessity of poetry.

Bill Mayer, author of *Longing, The Uncertainty Principle,* and *The Deleted Family*

Table of Contents

Bodysnatchers

1.
Each person now alive mirrors someone
who has died or is yet to be born. Walking
through museum galleries, you may find
in time a portrait of a face familiar as
your own, and in every crowded theater
you can descry a head like some ancient
noble's carved in stone. All snapshots plagiarize.
All life drawings limn ghosts. And angels
from the future find the bodies they desire
waiting for them like hosts in yours or mine.
A story told repeats itself someday, the dreams
of dreamers long dead recur, and memory,
obscure as an oracle, prophesies irresistible
events: Death's life, it says. It endlessly ends.

2.
So dreams' roots grow as fast as the simplest
cells divide. Too thirsty not to suck a body
dry, shoots slither through grates, climb
like tendrils over transoms, pierce walls,
carpeted floors to reach the beds where souls
lie sleeping. No baby is safe, crying at night,
unable to resist its illusions of life while roots
coil round its helpless body. Yet, in the morning,
snatched by aliens from a dying planet, children
pretend they know their mother, their father as
parents believe they see their true child. Dreams
root in whoever sleeps dangerously long.
Thereafter the world is not their home. To flower
by day was nothing. To flower by night is song.

Desert Warfare

Through the church's milky windows, the August noon light is sand-colored, like the cypress-rich, gritty Mayodan river banks not fifty feet away. Come, my heart says. His father reads from the lectern, his back to the choir. Seek his face. The church is bare-- plank floor, white-washed walls, from which no cross hangs, all images forbidden, idolatry despised, the worst of sins to see, in what man makes, God's hands or eyes. Though thunder storms, bush burns, never turn your face toward Him whom even Moses on his desert mountain top could not look upon and live. As his father preaches, the boy opens his sweaty palm. With the forefinger of the other hand, he invisibly sketches on its calloused skin God's handsome face as he imagines it, wavy hair, furrowed forehead, nose and jaw chiseled from stone. Though it's blasphemy, he likes to draw Jesus whenever he can. He stares back at his father who looks down at him as if he knows what his son's doing, his flesh gray as a gravestone as he prophesies the doom soon to come, the terrible end foretold for so many at that hour when only His precious few will be spared for Glory.

When war's declared, his dad is glad. Armageddon's even nearer than he's supposed, he warns his flock, the time nigh, the tribulation hastening. He sails for France to fight and drive the ungodly hordes of Huns from bloodied soil the battles have rendered desolate as a desert. His father gone, Leith draws everything he sees on every scrap of paper he can scavenge whether box top, torn envelopes, crumpled plain wrappers from gifts, or lined lesson books he steals from school, using charcoal saved from a hearth, chalk from a teacher's blackboard, pencil or pen bought with dimes he's earned and saved by doing chores. But every portrait he makes, every figure he draws, every bird he sketches he burns until the day he learns from his mother's tears he doesn't need to anymore. He's safe from his father's wrath. Does he feel no grief? His mother lacks even a photograph to remember him by until Leith, searching in his palm or in the air for all the drawings he's made of him before, paints with brush and ink a face she kisses every night before she goes to bed as if, without meaning to, in his portrait of him her son had brought her husband back to life.

From an older brother, Leith inherits an air rifle, good only for scaring squirrels and killing little birds. One winter Sunday afternoon, the sun so low it sets the tips of pine and oak on fire, lost, he stumbles into a clearing. Hazy smoke rises out of a riprap chimney. Carved from wood, painted birds peck for worms or perch on a bush twig or tree limb. He fears if he startles one, all will soar away. His lips gray as his beard, old Grover, once a potter, now a bird-carver, once a drunk wife-beater, now a recluse, wellknown outcast in these parts, eyes Leith as suspiciously as do his birds. His coveralls look cut to fit a person twice his weight. His lumbering feet shuffle in galoshes. His hat brim half hides or trims his bushy brows. Wood blocks, whittling knives, brushes lie on a table outside. Paint-smeared cans rest on their sides on a shelf. An unfinished crow waits on a slate slab. Uneasy, trying to back away, Leith clumsily knocks it over and steps on it, splitting it in two and splintering its head. He offers his brand new spit cleaned knife in payment for the bird he's ruined, but Grover, red-faced, refuses and, showing his fists, threatens him off his land. Leith escapes into the woods he just left where a crow caws at him angrily from a bobbing branch while other birds twitter, chirp, warble in their usual twilight choir. But this dusk their song sounds to Leith scary, prophetic, as if the half-finished wood bird he crushed belonged to their kind. He grips his rifle tighter and flees.

A ledge down to a creek flows into the river he follows home. In his room, Leith yanks off his muddy boots and sweat-damp socks and lies on his bed. He tries to pray but as usual no words come, and he falls fast asleep instead. Listen, son, his father says, the bible tells how you young men see visions while old men only dream dreams. But all you see is blasphemous. Look, your room is full of wooden birds. See, a field mouse dangles from an oaken barn owl's beak. A pine-born chicken scratches the earth beside a cherry quail. Only a flock of mock birds is chasing you, pecking at your arms and head. It's a mimic of creation. Nothing here is made by the Lord. But afraid anyway, Leith dashes into a meadow whitened by dogwood as if it were spring. As Grover's birds fly up and away, they circle the sky, filling its arc, twirling faster and faster in smaller and smaller rings until they burn as one, sun bright. But then, quick as a blink of God's eye, the light fails. It's all dark. Everything's empty in a nighttime moonless, starless sky. You're fixing to die young like me, his father says. Why?

In the morning, a tit mouse lands on a persimmon branch and, bobbing, cracks a seed, a flicker stares down at him from a tulip tree, a hawk spirals over an old oak stand, all laughing him awake. Go now, they say. It's time to quit your daddy's world. It's time to

5

create your own, find a God elsewhere who will let you be free. Leith grabs a bag, tosses in some clothes, a comb, a tooth brush, ties it closed, walks to where the river, grown lazily fat, curves so often a train bankside either slows to a stop or, braking too late, jumps the tracks. A black bull breaks through a fence and ambles onto the rails, looking at first light like a stalled Model A. It stops the train.

The empty boxcar smells barn stale. Leith lies against the bulkhead. The train jerks so hard it almost cracks his skull. As he rides the blind, cinders sting his skin like bees. The burning coal smells sulfurous. Second dawn, brakemen check the cars for bums. In Alabama, Leith scouts houses he can beg for food. By a water tower, up a dirt road, he waits for dark. An empty reefer carries him to Galveston. In a shelter, he showers and washes his clothes and sleeps on a cot with dozens of other waylaid men. In the morning, he hops a coal gondola that carries him to San Antone where railroad dicks catch him in a trap as he sneaks cross the yard. He reeks of coal and cows. After his release, a needle thin lady with a pink face offers him some iced tea and a pork sandwich which he devours as she reads to him from a devotional book his mother, too, had owned and quoted from so often he had memorized long passages. Two beatitudes and a long-winded prayer he recites earn him a slice of sweet potato pie.

Five miles from town, he skids down a sandy hill below a bridge into a dry river bed where ten men hover round a fire in an oil drum. Bricks, tin cans, car springs, hub caps litter the perimeter. Each star is moon bright in a tar black Texas night. While the men sleep, Leith sketches the pox scarred face of an old man, bony and worn, pig bristles sticking out his nose and ears. He looks dead to this world. When he wakes up, the likeness shocks him most of all.

A whistle blows two long blasts, one short. Sidetracked. A reefer hauls him to Barstow where he jumps on a boxcar that brings him to Frisco, land's end. In North Beach alley ways, he scrounges bakery waste bins for cake scraps or old bread. At the Y, he sketches from newspapers FDR, Cooper, Dietrich, DiMaggio and mounts them, each a portrait more true than the photographs from which they were drawn, on an old board he's hand sanded down. Behind an apartment, he finds two fold-up chairs and a stool. Ten cents a sketch, he charges, eight bits for one in ink--cheap, his sign announces, for such realism. A matron wearing beady eyed fox furs and a tiered black hat and a gent in a tipped bowler pay him five bucks. People are various as birds, he's often observed. He draws two plain sparrows--squat, round, and brown--their hair downy gray and rabbit soft. They wrap their thick necks in scarves. Her black skirt touches her toes. His trousers drag the walk. Because of the wind, she refuses to take off her hat. But her face is clear enough for him to draw anyway, despite the powder and half veil she wears to hide the blotches on her cheeks and jaw.

Their last assistant has just left their employment without notice, runaway to join the army. They offer him the job for a dollar a day. He agrees without dickering about more wages. After every morning's work, they take a long walk while Leith sweeps, washes, stacks, carries, wraps, unwraps this, that or hauls a barrel filled with wood and glass to the refuse bin. After two months, he learns to saw and carve simple frames, measuring, cutting, beveling, gluing, nailing the strips of wood he's prepared. Herr Braunfels rarely speaks but teaches by example, how to carve designs in frames, to flute wood strips, to use varnish, to gild, to cut mat and glass to fit each frame. No picture is so beautiful that it is not made more beautiful when beautifully framed, Herr Braunfels proudly proclaims. While Frau Braunfels cooks their evening meals, her husband reads aloud to him from brown volumes of German poetry or Luther's bible. Leith does not comprehend a word of either, but finds he can accept what God says better when he doesn't understand the meaning.

His free hours, Leith goes to double features with two cartoons and movietone news and imagines his father not killed in France but instead, long ago, a grown-up runaway like he is now, his dad for the time being a bit part player in movies on his certain path to stardom some day soon. That could be him standing just a foot away from Cagney, Muni, or Cary Grant. Or maybe he didn't ride the rails to Hollywood. Maybe he's that sailor racing off a gangplank of a ship just docked, back from the South China Sea. Or the guy in the red tie standing beneath the Ferry Building Clock or the warehouseman munching a burger at Pete's Eats on the corner of Fourth and Howard, eyes hardened to stone the way life will toughen a fellow sometimes. But not grown old, still the goodlooking man he was the day he left home. If, stripped of his Sunday preaching suit, his father should turn to look at him as Leith walks in to sit on a diner stool, no face in the world would surprise him less, not even the Lord's own.

Slow but steady, Herr Braunfels walks north toward the bay. Leith hesitates several feet behind him. Near the piers, the old man mounts a slight slope, rests on a bench, and stares at ships bound for the Pacific. Two sailors in their whites stroll past. A young couple lolls on the grass. A boy suns himself on a blanket. A ship's whistle blasts three times. Scared pigeons soar. Rainer is dead, Herr Braunfels says, killed in Russia. His blood has soaked the snow and the frozen ground below of that pitiless land. So far from home, the old man's niece still hears everything. In mourning, the Braunfels shut the shop for a week. Herr Braunfels lies listless on a sofa, smoking his clay pipe. Frau Braunfels works needlepoint or looks at one of her books, rich with color prints of religious paintings by German masters. She demands Leith study them with her, all the holy faces, she says, gripping his hand, so many, yet always so sad.

Surveying the piers, counting the ships that have docked during the day, he watches sailors and seamen his age or younger swarm toward Market and disappear in all directions. One night, he follows a tough blond guy and his three buddies to a saloon in an alley off Front. Two hookers sit on stools playing cards at the bar. In a corner, a redhaired soldier shoots a solitary game of pool. Huddled round a table near a window, the four sailors order chili and a bucket of brew. The girls join them, twirling strands of hair round their fingers and rubbing their knees against two guys' thighs. Leith slides off his stool. In another bar down the alley, he orders a shot. When the red-haired soldier walks in, he talks fast and saucy as a whore. At the shop, Leith forgets to lock and bolt the door behind them. We might have been killed, murdered in our sleep, Frau Braunfels shrieks the next morning. Good boys do not leave doors open to burglars at night. She cannot see the soldier from the bar retreat through a basement window onto the street. Leith packs his things into a cheap suitcase. At the door, for the trip home, Frau Braunfels offers him a bag of cold cooked sausages, fresh apple cookies, and a pocketful of nickels and dimes sticky with flour from her doughy hands.

At the bus station, he buys a ticket for L.A. Outside Glendale, he jumps a freight train east. As he lies on the hay strewn floor of an empty cattle car headed for Tulsa, he learns about Pearl Harbor from a tramp who's cracking walnut shells with his teeth. I'll fly away soon, the geezer says. The Good Book says we all will. He offers Leith a bite of the meat off his mud-encrusted mitts. Pins of sunlight prick Leith's eyes as the old timer, inspired by the spirit like his preacher daddy, lays his palms on him, muttering I baptize you, I baptize you, in the name of the only Lord, I baptize you. Again, like over two decades before, Leith's feet drag along the river's ford, his ears throbbing from so much song, the whole congregation gathered round him, thigh- or waist-deep in the sand-colored river, its bottom stirred up by recent storms. Stumbling on a rock, he splashes into the water before his father shoves him all the way under. His legs buckling, Leith slips on the slick bottom. There's no air, only river in his nostrils and mouth. He tries not to breathe, not to swallow. Baptism is our first death, his father would say, killing the sin in us so the saved part might live some day when our second death comes to fly us to heaven. Throwing his arms round his chest, his father hauls him back to life. Water drips down his face. Everyone is pressed too close, wanting to hug him or slap his back. His mother offers him a towel. But he sees no one, feels nothing. The Lord's face does not shine upon him as he watches the dove fly not down but up and further away. He shoves the old timer's hands off him. Somewhere close to Galveston, Leith hops off into a fallow field. Weeks later, in Laurel, Mississippi, tired of hitchhiking or walking days in the rain, Leith spends a night in jail for vagrancy. Early the next afternoon, he finds a recruitment office squeezed between a barber shop and a hardware store lined along a plank sidewalk so rotten and rickety no one could have taken saw or hammer to it for ages. It's only a miracle, the barber says, picking a tobacco speck off his tongue, that some good soul hasn't broken a leg.

After every battle, with his fingers, Leith sketches some dead man's face in the sand. But hot winds quickly blow the portraits away or snow-like drifts cover them over. He might be a fearful small boy again, secretly drawing in the air or on his palm faces no one, including himself, will ever see. Yet he draws them anyway. The desert wants to bury them all, of course, under dunes the winds sculpt naturally into graveyard mounds. As after a late summer thunderstorm back home, when the desert quiets, the sun throbs even hotter, more cruelly, rippling and fluttering the air until it bends and breaks and

9

splinters like glass. The sky is blindingly white. Even the pass where they'd just fought glares back at him blank as white paper, despite the unburied bodies splotching it like ink. Is it heaven or hell that dares him to stare harder, trying to read the marks as if they'd been written? He rubs his eyes and turns away to spare his eyes. He would like to sleep, but, at their sergeant's command, the men pick up their weapons and drag themselves forward toward the invisible line in the sand they're being told the enemy has recently drawn a few miles east, somewhere so empty, Leith already knows, it's past worth fighting over, past where the last birds can fly, close to where his father's God was born.

The Seventh Victim

The Room

Victorian: maroon upholstery, umber woodwork,
vast rose-rust velvet curtains to shield
the eyes of those inside from too much light.
They like the musty smell of rooms whose doors
are always closed. Brown out, war on:
gas lamps low. Like fungus, the smoke clings
to glass and plaster, unwashable. No matter
how hard maids scrape and wipe, they cannot
sweep away the dust that seeps through walls,
blows through thin panes. For which disgrace,
unbowed, the lady of the house will not apologize.
Her cat, porcelain black, arches its back
on a bookcase, leaps, creeps across a Persian
rug to claw, gold-surprised, on a thread of its pattern.

The Devotees

A woman in a silver sequined gown and mink
slinks behind a leather wing-back. Another
in a feathery hat nervously grips a small
beaded bag in her only hand. A frantically thin
blonde nibbles her fingers or fixes her hair.
A portly man in a tight three piece suit
sports a clerical collar and shines a quarter
on his vest. Sighing, his companion, dressed
in summer white, presses ice against
his forehead. Sitting beside an ormolu table,
fiddling with an ivory chess knight, a man
winks at the blonde who accepts from a tray
a cracker topped with paté. A clerk chimes
their names like time: Heart, Stomach, Sex,

Buttocks, Thighs, Hands, Liver. Feet takes
a sip of his sherry, spills some on Bowels'
minutes of the meeting when all had voted Soul
must die. Poor Bowels is a fretful speaker.
Blood-like spots soak into his papers.
Tongue started this trouble. She's dressed
shabbily again, only a beautician's assistant
until Soul had thrown her all she owned, like a bouquet.
Once more she jabs her finger menacingly
at her benefactor. "Us. She was talking about us."
Brains attempts to call them back to order.
A pince nez has pinched his nose for years.
With his knuckles, he knocks the lectern. "All
our secrets," she shrieks. He pounds the gavel. "Us!"

The Poison

My dear, do not miss the beauty of its liquid amber,
like fine brandy. Note how the cordial glass,
though smooth, breaks light like crystal into
the myriad colors of a Tiffany egg. Whiff it,
sweet. How gently it must tease the tongue,
how precious it must taste. The heretical monks
who make it age it for years in oak casques cut
from the Black Forest where alone it grows.
Because they know the secret of its antidote,
they imbibe it freely, without harm to their hearts,
and retire with due solemnity to their cells
to pray for lost souls. There's no liquor like it
in the world, they say. We envy you. With just
a swallow, you'll learn more than we'll ever know.

Hostias

Dressed in black, her page boy haircut
fuller than most, she raps her fingernails
against the lion's paw arm of her chair.
"No," she says. "No. No. No." Her nostrils
flare as the others point to the glass.
She wants to die. She's always wanted to
die, but will not if she's ordered to.
Their fear offends her. She's hung a noose
in her room. Each night, as hopefully
as her despair, she kicks the chair from under
her feet. It's graceful really, when death
works the rope-string of a puppet body
like a dancer's, the fall less a drop
than a leap, plié.

At the Metropolitan Opera

1.

How pleasant still to lounge in bed
when she is no longer ill at all,
her appetite appeased by sweet nut cakes
her mother bakes for her, the crumbs
pressed flat as petals by an old
book's pages. Ra-ta-plan, the soldiers
sing. Beneath cotton puff
mountain peaks, Marie waves
the tri-color and sings the Marseillaise
with the prettiest boys, the regiment dressed
in tinsel-tassel uniforms as flashy as those
adorning the toy warriors in the window
of Dorinda's favorite Christmas store.
Marie's no foundling after all
but daughter of nobility betrothed
to a handsome, shy Tyrolean
whose high Cs tease Dorinda,
too, seducing her quicker than kisses
would, reducing her to sighs like those
she's sure she'd breathe in a lover's arms.

2.

Dinorah stands among her father's goats,
singing to them her favorite goat songs,
daisies twined round her braided hair--
like her own, Dorinda notices, tugging
on one with fingers sticky from licorice.
Cow bells tinkle, like the cry of snow
at dawn as it begins to shift above
the goat herd's cabin in early spring.
Inside, her mother sews a lacy dress.

How sleepy she must feel, grown weary
of these mountains. Yawning, Dorinda
also counts how much of her girlhood
is left, wishing the years to come
to number no more than Dinorah's herd,
grazing for the summer in their pasture.
All this is mere prologue, Dorinda knows,
heard but not seen. As early as Act One,
in a valley darkened by war, Dinorah
will lose her last goat, her love, her mind
and sing a shadow song glacier-cold.

3.
Cio-cio-san stands in the middle
of the Bridge of Regret that curves over
the River of Sighs. Behind her lies
her girlhood, canebrake, and rushes
through which she's just passed, lovely
as calligraphy. A white heron glides
over head on the scrim, its flight
like the stroke of an artist's brush.
On the other side waits her womanhood,
the tea house, and the House of Pleasure.
An old man passes down the path,
a cricket cage dangling from a pole,
resting on his shoulder. "Go home,"
he warns. But Butterfly is already singing
her entrance aria and on the crest
above her her American sailor waits.
She's barely fifteen, just two years older
than Dorinda, who weeps at the end
of her story, fearful if men keep warring
Cio-cio-san's fate might be her own.

4.

Blackout. Shades drawn. Curtains
closed. Standing high above the others
startled out of their slumber by a frightened
doorman, Dorinda wakes to find
herself like Amina in La Sonnambula
walking on air. The church clock
strikes six. A policeman blows
his whistle. Though she can smell bread
baking and coffee brewing, she lifts
her skirt and climbs up a cloud as easily
as stairs. Her mother snaps, "How dare
you!" Her father orders, "Come down!"
Her brother cries, "Dorinda, I believe you!"
Too happy to reply, she smiles at heaven.
Her loosened hair streams bright
as the rising sun. Or bright as the moonlight
on the bridge she and her sweetheart
are crossing, her partner guiding each gliding
step upward like a dancer, holding her
gently while she executes her point work.

The Ghost Ship

Gertrud's a small woman with a Black Forest
contralto in the chorus at the Metropolitan.
When she sings solo, her sound's so chilly
listeners shudder, as at mist in the air, a fog
on the Hudson that makes two lonely people
riding the ferry clasp hands on the deck
by the railing: brume, brouillard, nebbia,
nebel, words cold as ghosts. She marries
because Dieter asks her. Eleven months after,
she gives him a daughter, fourteen years later
a son. She works as a seamstress in a Hoboken
shop and sings in the choir of Saint Matthew's
where her Erda alto soothes more souls
than the pastor can with all his Lutheran words.

While Dieter's painting a liner's hull in dry dock,
his son brings him the lunch bucket he forgot.
He sees his father's support rope snag, snap,
break. The fall bashes his brains in. His face
looks like a gutter drunk's. Ignoring the strikers,
the cops on the spot rule the death accidental.
Only sixteen, Eddie joins the Merchant Marines.
February twenty third, nineteen forty three,
near midnight, Germans torpedo his freighter
in the North Atlantic. All twenty three of the crew
and their ship are lost. Just the day before,
Eddie had turned twenty three. His birthday
had doomed her son. On his cenotaph, Gertrud
orders his name but no dates be inscribed.

Her fingers now tremble too much for her
to work needle or thimble. Her sight's bleary.
She drinks in a saloon at a table Hans Sachs
might have used to cobble his shoes, stares
over piers toward ships' lights as they enter
or leave the harbor, waiting for Eddie, his black
freighter, the one her weak eyes spy nightly
on the horizon skating a sea ice-white and -slick,
some day perhaps to sail up river. Under
a bright moon, his ship will cast no shadow
and drift like a ghost ship with no hope of port.
Her mother scowls at her, her father beams,
Dieter winks. Her loved undead fill the room.
Her sister sits across from her, her silliest

hat on her head as she croons her silliest
Swabian tunes. Aunt Sophie says not a word,
nursing her beer while her older brother
smokes in a corner, the smell of his pipe,
though strong, cherry ripe or sweetly apple.
Of those she mourns, all show except Eddie.
One night, weeping, she follows a foghorn to
two ships berthed side by side. Sirens from
a fire truck blocks away pierce the mist
like sun rays breaking through rain clouds.
In that shrill gleam, like a tenor's high C's,
she sees her son on the dock. His tears mock
her fear away. Lights from a ship churning
eastward glow, dim, then, like him, disappear.

Or was it only a pipe's red embers she saw?
A heavy wool sweater, a sailor's cap? She looks
for the man, but trips on a strand of coiled rope.
The ship's rigging's dripping like trees after rain.
The man's beard, though soiled, is snowy.
She walks toward the gangplank. The ship's
whistle is plaintively woody. A bustle in the wings.
The cast approaches to assume their roles
before the curtain rises. Chains rattle and clang.
Someone calls out, "Places." Hers is with the women
in the spinning chorus. The stage is moving
like a true ship this time, cutting the current.
The river laps against the hull. Iron stairs
lead into a hole. The steps are slippery,

the railing Arctic cold. She loses her footing.
The walls are frigid. In a small room, the crew
lie on bunks or in hammocks, their blankets white
with rime. Whatever she touches, the metal
crumbles, rusty, rotted. Weakly, she climbs
the stairs feeling as cursed as the Dutchman she,
like Senta, longs for. When she grabs the rungs
of a ladder, the bridge rolls to port. A red light
blinks over the crow's nest. As the ship lists more,
she loses her grip. The deck's too slick to stand on.
She skids into the lifelines. Her coat and dress
might have saved her if the cords her clothes
wrap round had not been so dangerously frayed.
The water's too icy to swim in. Dying, she prays.

Home's a narrow, sooty, old brick house,
identical to others squeezed side by side
down block after block. Beneath the odor
of lilac sachet, next to the kitchen, the parlor
smells of sausages cooking and turnip soup.
The purple velvet curtains are closed halfway.
Yet long shadows fall across the furniture
and floor, cast by porcelain vases, crockery jars,
bronze urns. The woodwork's as dark
as German bock. Framed in silver, Eddie's
photograph hangs over a black chest.
His yellow hair, sharp nose, glacier blue eyes
are his mother's pride, as his hard jaw
had been his father's. Upstairs, Gertrud lies

under a thick afghan she knit herself.
Her head rests stone still on an unwrinkled,
embroidered pillow case. The sea, the Atlantic,
had been deadly cold, its waves heaven-high.
She'd seen the freighter, Eddie swimming beside
it. He'd caught her. He'd stood up and walked
on that water, he'd leaned over and lifted her
up out of danger to hold her in his arms
and carry her here. Is it snowing? Gertrud
can't see through the lace curtains her daughter
refuses to part. The watchman saved her when
she fell in, Pastor Dieskau says. Tipsy, she'd tripped
on some rope, no doubt. The pastor's hat ill fits
his puffed up dumpling head bobbing like a toy.

After he's gone, Gertrud feels dreadfully cold,
as if another great wave had broken over her.
The snow swirls in the wind. The thin panes
rattle and crack. At first blurry glance, she thinks
the darkness approaching her is just the black
bough of the locust the storm's bent closer.
But as it hovers nearer she sees it's the hull
of a vast captainless freighter, slowly turning
toward her bed through thick blinding snow
and gale swept churning waves. As the bow
rams through the walls, icy fingers, stronger
than Eddie's, grip her arm to save her again.
The crew sings the storm-wind music the ocean
knows from Wagner's score. She isn't afraid.

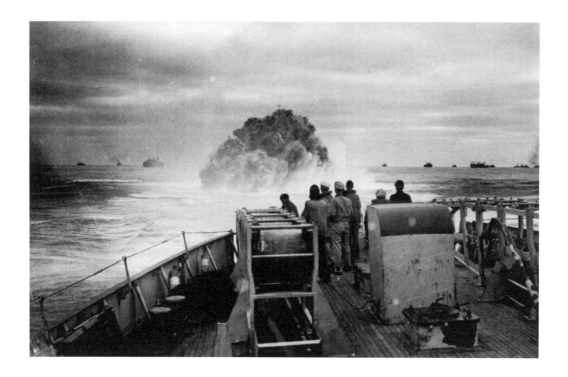

Give Us Peace

A converted mansion, the Home was built on flat farmland: sparse windows, black oak molding, paneling, wainscoting, no carpets on hard floors, no flowers, no decorative pictures, no paintings allowed, all profane, worldly, ungodly scenes forbidden. A black slate roof is capped by a bell tower that narrows to a steeple's sharp point. A curving thick brick wall borders a horseshoe drive. Each spring, when the grounds flood, debris dragged from ragged upriver farms litters the yard. During the storms, Ned hears the walls talk. Like an insomniac, he glares at bare boards and swears ghosts sigh through windy cracks or chinks in the chimney.

In Mrs. Kittle's office, Alice clicks on the radio, prays the war won't last another year. For Jesse's sake, she stays vigilant, listens to reports of every battle fought in France. Though she refuses to recall her dreams, they hurt her bad all day. The rain has turned to sleet, the sleet to ice, buckling trees and bushes. Pole wires sag. She pronounces with the announcer Caen, Saint Lô, Aachen, the Ardennes. Then checks on Ned, gazing out the window, to him one season much the same as any other. The river rises or falls, the birds soar away or fly back, the brick wall crumbles more, an old cedar grows taller, its boldest limbs touching his sill with their fingers. She undresses him, slips on his night shirt, carries him, so light he might be her child, to bed. He vows he never sleeps, fearful of the little boy inside his head who begs him to save him from the dark. Childless, he sometimes talks about his young son fighting in the Pacific. "Peaceful," she says to comfort families when they ask how kin die in the Home. "Peaceful." But she knows, if Jesse has been killed since his last letter, he hasn't died peacefully. Few people ever do. Not even Jesus did. She tucks Ned into his unmade bed, begs him not to tell her his dreams again, leaving always unsaid her fear of her own.

In the blank dark, Ned again watches his younger brothers run away, through with mucking barns, slopping hogs, spreading manure. In his store, he'd sold hard candy, chews, snuff tins, cotton bolts, jeans, shoes, boots, mugs, jugs, earthenware plates, hammers, saws, levels, ladders, bright glass beads, paper flowers, wax fruit, straw hats, their bands either yellow or red. In time, the aisles lengthened, narrowed, the store smelled musty as an attic, stinging noses like dust blown off a fallow pasture. On his eightieth birthday, a preacher pinned a medal on his lapel because he'd never missed a Sunday or Wednesday night in over sixty years. Try as he might, he can't recall falling the next morning between a pile of tin buckets and a pot display, his scalp bleeding from a gash it took when it bashed the counter. He feels sorry for the birds and squirrels whose nature compels them to live all winter in snow. In newspaper photos, soldiers march under bent trees, their faces glassy with ice. His room smells like the liver pills he'd sold. His bones feel sharp enough to slice through his skin. Lights on, Alice offers him a chew and wipes off a resin-colored crust that's formed round his nostrils and teary eyes.

Ned's favorite time of day is dawn, not for the sun it promises but the light it discreetly holds back while he's stripped, made to pee, sponge bathed, shaved, dressed, brushed, combed. His pants and shirt droop off him like a child playing in grown-up's clothes. Suddenly tired of it all, the time he spends each day and night uselessly dying, getting nowhere, he picks his walking sticks off the floor, sneaks down the hall past Alice distracted by her radio, and wanders out the door, unnoticed, free. But his sticks crisscross on the sidewalk, his legs buckle. A hum like the river's sings in his head and curves lazily away, like a boy on his bike. The nurse's hands, picking him up, are so kind he sobs at her touch. You could have broken your hip, Mrs. Kittle scolds him back in his bed. He tugs on his thin white hair, purses his lips, despairs. Will he ever walk again, with sticks or without? Alice expresses no doubt and tells him again the story of how she and Jesse, lost after running out of gas driving off the road the south slope of High Rock, had stumbled out of the woods into a moonlit clearing just after Jess had spent his last match. Back for boot camp just before shipping out, he sang her a bawdy ballad while he tinkered with his truck. Alice sings it to Ned, humming the words to the naughtier parts.

After lights out, Alice refolds Jesse's letter, weeks old, along its creases and tucks it back into a pocket of her uniform. The Home's perpetual dark frightens her. Not even by day, after she's drawn back the curtains and lifted the shades, does sunlight ever brighten its halls and rooms. Once she's heard enough of the news on the radio, she moves from room to room, against the rules clicking some lamps back on, longing to be surprised by some attractive print hanging on a wall, a rug with an arresting pattern, flowers in a lovely vase. The war must be over soon. It must. Outside, the lawn sparkles like salt. As a full moon lifts over the old oak grove, patches of the white world below gleam like her mother's porcelain set on her shiny, silver-threaded linen cloth--the one she promised her after Jesse proposed.

Anxious, drawn, Alice is spending too much of the morning in Ida Kittle's office, listening to new reports. Down the hall, Maud Swindle thumps her cane on the floor. Ida calls to Alice from her door. So weak he can no longer sit, Ned is staring out his window. Alice sneaks in and sits next to him to hold his hand. They could be two good children minding each other on a park bench or a pew in church. "The Lord shine his face on us," Ida Kittle murmurs, "and give us...." She couldn't finish. Overcome, she retreats to her office. Sixty-six, yet she still misses the wrapped baubles her mother would leave at night on her chest of drawers, the hard candy treats her father brought her home from work, warm and sticky from his fist.

Seven from His Flock

1.

Maybe her father did forbid her to marry,
the boy's skin darker than hers. Maybe
that shot from his pistol missed its mark.
Maybe her brother's hate for them both

is a hell a convent can save her from.
What's done is done. God knows, the girl's
no nun. But in the midst of a war bloodier
still can anything this bloody turn out well?

2.

Her brother's wounds have never healed.
Good Friday, noon, her eyes bleary,
Sue slices her palms with a paring knife.
Our Lord mixed mud with spittle to dab

on a blind man's eyes. Barry rubs her
blood on his festering scars like a balm
a doctor's prescribed, his pain unrelieved
by a miracle he'd ached to believe in.

3.

At her drag shows, she bills herself as Consuelo
Canswallow and brags how God made her balls
like a bull's. She loves Jesus but hates his dope
of a pope, Pius the coward. In church, she hides

in a back corner, behind a column. Her man's
a shipyard worker whose greasy hands betray
a telltale pattern on her dress. Without mass,
she'd be lost. She sucks the host like candy.

4.

Born armless, her face as pretty as Grable's,
Alissa's never worked, never married.
Her mother believes a crippled witch's
mal occhio withered her daughter's limbs

in her womb to steal them for her own.
To me, she repents of feeling trapped
in a loveless body, as in a confessional
whose door a priest must open for her.

5.

Each Friday, after Sean quits hauling trash
off Flatbush streets, he buys a bookie a beer
at a bar in exchange for hot tips on the ponies
at Vernon Downs upstate. He always loses.

On Sundays, he bets on the Yankees he loves
or the Giants he hates, choosing his lucky
numbers from the number of sins the priest cites
in his homily that morning. He never wins.

6.

Christmas Eve, Connor slips off a snowpacked
roof where he'd been told not to play
five stories to his death. At midnight mass,
his father sneaks an ice pick from his jacket

and stabs Jesus where he lies in his creche,
screaming over and over to the splintering
wooden baby, "Bleed, you mean son
of a bitch. You heartless bastard, bleed!"

7.
Anna Nini believes God is gravity
and she a wave falling and rising
between earth and moon
until she breaks upon a shore.

"No more Anna Nini," she says,
tap-tapping her World's
Fair spoon against
an empty coffee cup.

Three Day Leave

Gulls strut on the dock. His fresh blue shirt
spangling in sunlight, Curt, sweating,
coils hawser round bollard. When his crotch
itches, he scratches it. A tug nudges
a sludge barge up river. Train-flats,
two freighters, and a fireboat glide past.
Chain pulleys carrying supplies clatter
shipside as swarming men on deck funnel
down flanks to the pier, racing toward shore.

He spit shines his shoes to a bootblack's pride.
His fresh whites stick to his skin. In a small
steel mirror, he checks the tilt of his hat
on his head. He flips open his wallet, counts
the bills. He salutes smartly four times
before he steps back on land. Times Square
lures him like a pulp book cover. A barker
wearing a weather-worn, snap-brim
fedora tugs on the sleeves of two marines.

Globes hang in a triad of a honky tonk bar
where soldiers sing, "Who Wouldn't Love You."
Across the street, G.I.s fire rifles at metal targets
in a shooting gallery. Two whores wearing short
yellow skirts stroll past, their arms linked,
their heels clicking on the sidewalk. The hot night
sweats. Close to Third Avenue, he stops
where the sidewalk and the street are slashed
by slats of light from a window in which a sign

reads, Cheap Rates. By Day. By Week. On the El,
a train screaks past. The clerk is thin as light
at dusk. He studies the blocks pencilled in
on a large torn paper sheet, slips Curt a key.
The elevator doesn't work. From the sixth floor
stairwell, he hears shouts, curses, laughter.
His room's door's wide open. Two sailors
are playing cards. Curt drops his sack
against the wall of a bed where a big guy

in his skivvies smokes a cigar, a glass ashtray
nestled in the black mat of his chest hair.
When Curt tells him his name, the guy barks it back.
In the john, as his piss floods the urinal, he reads
numbers and names etched and scrawled
on the crumbling wall and studies the crude
pencil sketches. He hears a torpedo hit
below the waterline. After the last blast, the ship
sinks slowly until his brain is empty again.

In the morning, Curt showers in a rusted stall,
dresses, escapes. Under the shadows of the tracks
of the elevated railway, he eats an orange he's cut
with his penknife, picking out the seeds with the blade.
An ancient Chinese woman in slip-slop slippers
passes a young woman wearing a blue cotton
frock and Minnie Mouse white high heel shoes.
In the air, he sniffs grease, smoke, malt. The bars
are as packed as troop trains. He walks west,

then north toward the park. Down narrow streets,
delivery trucks rumble and reverberate. Fleshy women
sit on stoops of smoky brownstones, sipping
the sun. At the streetlight, Curt watches the driver
of a wing-fendered Checker cab curse the stooped
driver of an old hansom. In the park, children are flying
kites. Four fat, grizzled men toss horseshoes.
Dressed in a white suit like those men wear
in hot places in movies, his face ax-head thin,

a man approaches him. His sharp chin juts out
as he jangles change. Curt arches his back, yawns.
The man smiles like a child half asleep, steps
closer, crooking his right eyebrow warily. Two boys
dash past them on bikes. A taxi stops at the curb
and lets out a woman whose gold watch flashes
in the sun. His building is five blocks away.
When they reach his bedroom, the man nuzzles
Curt's offered neck. Like blind men, their fingers

read each other's bodies. They undress slowly,
but, once naked, rush into each other like water
into a ruptured hull. Back outside, Curt fixes
his bucket hat on his head, tugs on his neckerchief.
The sun burns his eyes. The air feels wet and salty.
There's plenty of leave left. As he reaches Times
Square his heart pounds, and he struggles for breath.
Like a swimmer who's gone out too far, he's caught
in tides which sweep him still further from shore.

The night is stubborn, the stars like pins. He squats
by the shore-end of the pier and watches another
trick disappear behind the crates and boxes that hid
them from the streetlight. A police boat churns
the dark river. Water slaps at the piles. Flecks
of black clouds smudge the sky lit by a crescent moon.
He refastens his bell bottoms' buttons and wipes
his lips. Near the ocean, a ship's siren sounds.
He brushes himself off and heads for a Broadway bar.

Back in the cheap hotel where he's bunking,
dead drunk, he collapses on a cot and props
his head on a pillow, trying in the midst of a whirl
to see what's happening. He labors to focus
on a rust-colored water stain, on the light bulb
dangling from a quivering cord. His old pocket-knife
is digging into his skin. He pulls it out and drops
it on the floor. Someone forces him to drink
some more while a muscle guy holds his nose.

Curt fights for breath to keep from drowning.
The first blows sound far away, like distant
gunfire. He tries to get out of bed. He wants
to raise his hand to stop it or to try to cry out.
As he labors to hook a buddy out of oil-slicked
water, his body squeaks like wet rubber.
No one screams. It's all fuzzy. The eyes he sees
are dull as scratched marbles and he hears nothing
except weeds being slowly ripped or uprooted.

Bile and phlegm clog his throat. His stomach feels
clotted with rot from harbor stews. A distant roar
of waves fades in his ears. His tongue tastes of brass
and acid, like spoiled tomatoes. He smells blood.
In the hall, someone falls against the door and barfs.
The light on the ceiling from the window is gun
barrel gray. A body lies on the floor between the beds.
The big guy with the hairy chest. Drool trickles
down his chin like snail slick. Rust-colored stains

streak the sheet which binds his naked body.
His ears have been sliced, his prick split
down its shaft. From his heart rises the mother-of-pearl
handle of Curt's penknife plunged into a pool
of blood. With a pillow case, he wipes away
the lick spittle from his face, closes the bulging eyes,
grabs his bag, and darts from the room. Trying not
to run, he heads for Times Square. By noon, he's standing
in line at the depot, disguised in stolen civvies.

The fourth morning a.w.o.l, he wakes to a train's
whistle filling the sky like the sun at dawn
while the bus somewhere in the plains waits
for passengers to return from breakfast
at a rest stop. Beside a copse of spindly, silvery
trees, a Nash with sidewall tries and wheelshields
idles empty. Curt reaches for his pack from the rack,
rushes up the aisle, and jumps down onto
the hard packed dirt. The driver stifles a yawn.

The Nash's door's unlocked. Even as he drives off,
nobody dashes out of the restaurant to chase him.
The seat beside him is covered with maps. The wind
dries the sweat off his face. He keeps to back roads
and sleeps in the breaks between boredom and fear.
Near the desert, the first rain begins, the lightning
like sheets of foil unrolling in the sky. He pulls off
at a diner where he sits in a booth beneath a row
of buzzing lights, his coffee cup shoved aside,

and rests his elbows on a tabletop too shiny for his eyes.
Rain splatters the plate glass window to his right.
A guy with a broom picks a nickel off the floor
and slips it into the jukebox slot. Winds slap
the roadside sign. Cops stomp in, dripping wet,
and hook their hats and jackets onto a rack.
He places a quarter onto the saucer. As he drives off,
no one notices him leaving. Through the desert,
the windshield wipers go click-clack, click-clack.

He crosses a mountain pass, barely able to see
through the rain to the road's edge. At one sharp curve,
the guard rail's red reflectors flare. He brakes
and, skidding, quickly turns. Near the border,
barricades have been set up, but he doesn't think
they are searching for him. It is only a detour,
directing him a different way. When he reaches
a town, the sky's clear, the moon bright.
At the plain, cheap hotel he pays in advance.

Having locked the door, he rests on a bed
too soft for his body but blessed with a view
of the river from where his head lies, the shade
pulled up so that he can almost see the water
rushing over rocks and the dark woods
where owl, wildcat, shrew, mouse, and bat
perform their nightly rites. In the morning,
he sits on the porch, eating eggs and ham.
A groggy lizard slithers across stones.

In less than a day, he could be at the ocean,
free. In the morning, he steers the Nash like a sailboat
driven by strong winds. Green fields flow past.
At a roadside stand, he stops to buy oranges.
When he searches in his pocket for his knife,
panic scratches his heart. He tears at the orange's
skin and sucks it dry. Through sleepy towns,
he slows to a crawl. In a valley of flowers, a boy
stands by a eucalyptus, a straw hat tipped

on his head, his dungarees too big for him, his thumb
held out. Curt breaks for him. As the boy runs
toward the car, Curt mutters to himself,
That could be me almost, a few years back.
The boy slumps in his seat as Curt cuts
onto the road. They ride in silence through orchards.
The citrus smell etches like acid in the air.
A flock of blackbirds swoops down into a field.
The boy rests his head on the seat and gazes

at the car's ceiling. "I've been drafted." He swallows
the saliva in his mouth. "I'm going to die.
I know I'm going to die." Dogs on the porch
of a bungalow bark at them as they pass.
Once in the city, Curt asks directions from a parking lot
attendant to a cheap hotel. Their room stinks
of fish. Curt opens a window. Outside, pigeons coo,
their coral claws fixed as if snagged on the fire
escape. Webs weave patterns in cornices.

In the morning, Curt wakes first and slips on
the boy's briefs, socks, shirt, dungarees.
Even his boots fit. The boy's muscles ripple
as he stretches, yawns. Curt smiles. "How do I look?"
The boy rubs his eyes. "You wouldn't fool my mom."
"I don't need to fool her. Just some dumb sergeant."
"You're going to die." "Yeah," Curt says. "I know."
Puzzled, the boy says, "You want to die?" Curt
fixes the boy's straw hat on his own head. "No."

Angaur. Peliliu, honey-combed with natural caves
that face each other across sheer gorges,
their entrances sealed by concrete blast walls
or oil drums filled with coral. Mangled corpses
spew out across shallows. Leyte. Ormoc Valley
where storms turn day into night. He slithers and slips
from one steep muddy slope to another, from ridge
to ridge where mountain meets sea. Men are bled
white. Like bread or cracker bits scattered for birds,

they lie on ground soggy and bloated from rain.
A bridge explodes. Flames billow from pillboxes.
Luzon. Each trail bend exposes more jungle.
In the mountains, the thunder is manmade. Afraid,
they hide in empty caves. His stools are bleached as bones.
Though dizzy from disease, he sees the trigger wire
concealed in an overgrown path to an old stone bridge
and safely guides his men around it to a stream
where flocks of birds flap their wings and squawk
                    like sullen gulls.

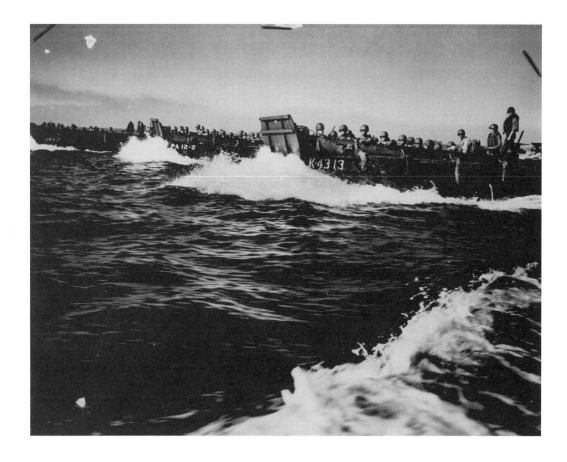

Photographer

George loves George, the boy's face bulldog
blunt, tough, hungry--a kid's mug
in a Weegee shot pressed against a window
by a rough crowd waiting in line at a soup
kitchen. His own looks are incised, intaglio,
etched like Sitwell's in his picture of her:
a pale aristocrat in a Tudor miniature.
His art plies tricks of light, shadows. He shoots
George nude, his privates gauze-shaded, not
invisible. Before he leaves for France,
George brings his kid brother to the studio.
After he's killed, his lover dresses Jonathan
in an army uniform. For the shoot, the boy
bows his head to hide his features. His boots

glow like a saint's face. There's a picture in
the picture: George, sixteen, resting his jaw
on his fist, almost smiling. To one side of it,
a square, to the other a rectangle, abstractions
as blank as the floor where George's headshot
floats, hovers, almost sinks until saved by
this print the photographer makes of brother
impersonating brother. George loves George.
Yes, and loves Jonathan, too, dressed in
his uniform. Magic in a camera's click: George,
Jonathan, his body double, mimicking what
only the lens can see so a man might love,
mourn, this brother, that brother, this lover, that
lover, this one, that one, the same the same.

Unfit to Serve

Four for the price of three, his own uncarved,
smoothly polished. The rest watch over the bed
of his dead, their names, chiseled into granite,
dark like a faded tattoo. Doctors scare him
worse than rattlers, more than the gobs of black
blood he coughs up each morning. Glory
is easy for those not ill. Without labor, they shine.
Even by the light of full day, his eyes hide
in shadows like bats in the back of caves.
Neither father, son, nor holy ghost is fair.
Al's dull, his mama said. His teachers left him
alone. Drafted, he stood six feet four,
weighed one hundred thirty. Questioned, he stuttered.
Poked, prodded, he fainted. Unfit to serve.

At the soda fountain, his boss picks on him.
His supper's a can of soup, egg whipped in,
poured over bread. A Dr. Pepper. A hunk
of cheese. Honeysuckle clings to the house
a foot deep, its scent so strong it's yellowed
the plaster. But an orange is sweeter than
honeysuckle on his tongue. Summer thick
with salt, like skin, the salty sweet taste of skin
untasted the best taste of all. At dawn,
the air ripples, the soil's sun-white, the sky
a blue glaze. Sharp grass, frazzled leaves.
Drawn shades, blinds, drapes. The heat hits
like a wall, steel-strong. Afternoon, dark clouds
billow from a blaze somewhere. The sky's gun-

metal gray. The oily air gleams yellow.
Loose twigs, dead leaves fall like stripped-off
shorts. The rain pounds his roof hard as pebbles.
The roads run blood-red from the clay. At dusk,
the earth steams white like smoke from a dying
fire. Porch swings creak. Moths cling to screens.
Tires splatter the shoulders. Al pushes his bed
to the window, lies naked on a naked mattress,
gazes at the moon. Nights are a tunnel, an under-
ground cave, a hole to hide in. Bat cry, owl cry.
The buzz of bugs on the screen. Leaves rustling
in the unquiet breeze. If lights were on across
the street in Deana's room, he'd stand on a chair
to see the blond hairs on her arms glistening

as she lays clothes out for morning. The rasp
of the cicadas's hotter than air. Al can't find
the moon for the trees. Red-eyed, a possum
stares at him like the gun that blew his daddy's
brains out. The fireflies' flickering scratches
his eyes. When the coughing returns, Al's spit
is pink and stinks like a turd. Your bed or mine?
Mine, his father says. He's heard this story
before, prefers the other in his head, Deana
and him years hence, shooting the breeze,
playing cards, listening to 78s or the short
wave, talking about their kids, him bragging
how it's all turned out just fine ever since
he almost died taking the beach at Anzio.

Gift Giver

As the earth steams, dark clouds rumble. Cicada chirr, flies and bees buzz, lake frogs croak, tree frogs throb, birds twitter, chirp, spin melodies all in choir, prophesying the storm to come. No need to plant flowers in a garden when the Lord roots his bounty in the woods behind her home. A summer thunderstorm is grace enough. When Jeff's mother darns or sews, each stitch she makes takes her a step further on salvation's path. If her people should hunger, the Lord will conjure stones into bread. If they should sorrow, He will turn their tears into pearls. Listening to their fears, He hears all their doubts like hymns of praise. Once He sacrificed His son on love's cross, what more will he give if not life forever and a day.

Woodsville is a solitary place. Most make do with what they grow and sell or market in town. Bad times make life not hard but harder. Tribulation is a test of faith. She cooks for everyone she can, shares more than she can spare. Her husband's daddy built their house. The roof tilts east, the porch west. But butterfly bushes cover the windows better than curtains, and wild rose clings to the clapboard like paint.

Her son Jeff's a good boy. He gives away his lunch at school to any child of the grimy Inmann clan or to poor Fanny Merridale whose ragged daddy died of consumption and drink. Sooner or later, some sickly kid is writing with Jeff's pen or wearing his scarf, cap, gloves, or galoshes. He gave Terry Inmann his best fishing pole and a can of fresh worms, Randy his favorite rifle, Taylor his Sunday shoes. He sleeps with his dog, feeds him with more than scraps from his plate. With every step he takes, she is sure he grows in stature with the Lord, but with every gift he gives for kindness's sake she knows he glows more handsome in the eyes of man.

Her husband's strong, clever, faithful hands can fix everything. The Good Book is all he needs to read, one verse at a time, though he knows a dozen psalms by heart. But when the war comes to Woodsville there's nothing anyone can do but pray. Amos bawls before he leaves to drive their son to meet his bus at the stop on Route 29. As the door opens, Jeff waves and promises them he won't get killed. His mother makes such a display she trembles she's ruining his day. In church on Sunday, Steve Ebert tells them he's lost his son Bud on Kwajalein but will grieve for him only as long as Jesus wept for Lazarus. What God has given is his to take. Praise, they all say, to the Lord.

Five months after the Japs surrender, Jeff finds himself in Frisco on his way home, still a soldier if not for much longer. He meets Ray in a bar popular with the Presidio quartermaster's corps Ray had served in, too noisy to talk and so crowded they are told they have to share a table with seven others who choose to ignore them. When Ray asks to bum a smoke, Jeff gives him the whole pack and offers him the silver-plated lighter a bullet had dented on Luzon. Ray slides it back across the beer slick table. His car's parked outside, two blocks away. Inside Ray's apartment, the one he'd rented on Telegraph Hill during the war, Jeff touches things he's heard of but never seen before-- oil paintings, copper urns, porcelain Chinese vases, velvet curtains, stained glass lampshades, Ray's battered lacrosse stick hanging over his bed, a model sailboat on his desk. Ray's sleeping it off on a couch, snoring gruffly, his scotch spilled on a rug where his cigarette still smolders, burning a hole in a rug. Jeff douses it out, rips a slip of paper from a pad, finds a pen by the phone, prints in caps his address back home, and stuffs it in Ray's khaki trousers. In the early morning light, his sweaty chest hairs, sparkling like wet black sand, make Jeff too nervous for him to stay for the breakfast Ray had promised to cook like a five star chef, neither having eaten a bite all night.

Home less than a week, Jeff finds a job. He doesn't mind the hours. In the army, at boot camp, he liked to wake first, listening to men breathing in the dark. He rarely sleeps much anyway. He got out of the habit on the islands. He lives in his old house with his parents. His milkman's route covers half of Woodsville and all of Zion Bible College. Should his buddy Ted's wife get sick or the kids keep him at home, Jeff substitutes for him and works twice as fast. At the annual picnic, Jeff's a good sport and never's lost the three legged race five years in the running. At pickup baseball, he's a decent hitter, though better at left field. Every Sunday at church, he sneaks a ten in the collection plate his father passes to him without a word.

When the preacher catches her Amos fondling Sally Pritchett's breasts in the bible school parking lot, Jeff's mother knows that her life is over. They give their house to Jeff and move two counties west where no one knows them. Whenever he visits them in their shabby rooms over the dress shop, his dad won't look at him while his mother hides in the kitchen, worrying over a lunch or supper no one much feels like eating.

Climbing the steps of All Holiness Church on the first Sunday in December, Amos grabs his head like God's wrath has struck, topples over, and tumbles down to the curb. Some believe at first, unsteady on his feet as he often is from the sin of drink, he's slid on the slick steps. But when he fails to move or breathe they whisper, Stroke. They all saw it coming. At the grave, Jeff's mother prays loud enough for the deaf to hear that the Lord forgive her these long days and nights she's hated the man. At the Pentecostal Home, she enjoys the company and doesn't complain, not even after she's broken her hip. She shares her room with a bald, toothless woman who curls naked in her bed like a starving baby. When he visits, Jeff scents both of their cheeks and necks with rose water and offers them a bauble or a broach he's bought at the five and dime where the clerk likes to tease him about the girlfriend he's always buying trinkets for.

New flurries are falling as Jeff walks to his milk truck. A kitchen light dims behind him. The wind howls. A door slams. As he reaches where he's parked, he sees him, too tall to hide, bending down in back of the empty crates. Despite the cold, the motor turns over quick, but the truck skids on the ice of an unlit road. His route done, he drives slow the rest of the way to the dairy where his pickup's waiting. Jeff opens the door for him and asks him to sit. The kid says his name's E.A. and tells him his story, three weeks on the road, a runaway from Arkansas and a dad real quick with a whip or the back of his hand. Jeff puts him up in his parents' old bedroom. His clothes will fit him good enough at first. He fries them both a chuck burger they greedily devour.

Next day, E.A.'s hired at Moser's General Store. At the town variety shop, Jeff buys him five white shirts and two pair of slacks. Hearing its mewing from the truck, he rescues a cat from a garbage bin, but, let loose at his home, she's chased by wild dogs in the woods where E.A. finds her after dark shivering in an oak bough, soaked from a storm. The chill kills her. In the morning, Jeff buries her in what's left of his mother's old sweet potato patch.

Out of the blue, seven years late, Ray writes he wants to see a Southern fall, autumn as it's meant to be outside of sunny coastal California. For his visit, Jeff picks wild roses in the woods and sticks them into colored pop bottles. When he drives up, on time to the hour, Ray parks his spiffy MG behind Jeff's pickup. He's wearing a loose white t-shirt, jeans, loafers. His big hands are always moving, touching things. When he stretches, he almost splits his clothes. After such a long journey, he says he's eager for exercise. Ray, Jeff, and E.A. take the long way round the hill where the woods open onto Big Pine Lake at their feet. Ray dips his hands into the water, smiles, strips. As the cold water reaches high up his thighs, his showy muscles tighten, his studly cock dwindles. Stripping too, E.A. follows him in. Swim over, they shower together while Jeff cooks dinner. After they've eaten, Ray wants some entertainment. The closest picture show is two towns east. Jeff wakes by three six days a week. Don't mind him, he says. When they've left without him, he watches TV. At ten, he clicks off the porch light. At dawn, Ray and E.A. are still gone. Jeff lies and calls in sick to work.

Late that afternoon, when E.A.'s boots finally clomp across the porch, Jeff tastes metal on his tongue, sharp as iron, salty as blood, and tries to swallow it, but it won't go away. He knows the story without having to be told. The sheet barely covers his nakedness as he rolls out of his swaybacked mattress to take his soldier's watch from the dresser. When E.A. enters his room, he straps it on his wrist and fastens the clasp. A good fit, probably safer on his than Jeff's own wrist. As Ray and E.A. prepare to leave, Jeff wanders the woods, picking berry sprigs for luck as his mama would, the trees' canopy enough shelter for him to weather the downpour until they've disappeared from his life before dark.

At work, though Ted asks him how he's feeling, he says nothing. E.A.'s his cousin on his mother's side, he'd told them all. Now he tells them he's gone back home to Arkansas. Jeff's mother dies in May. He thinks about quitting his job and selling the house but cannot imagine where he would go instead. No church goer, E.A. let Jeff attend alone. But the last time he worships there is when he watches his mother laid in the grave he'd helped dig himself, her bones now forever three counties removed from the husband she'd loved long and hard before she loathed him. May heaven reconcile them, Preacher Hayes says to him, slapping his back. Jeff lays a bouquet of wild roses by her headstone.

He's walking down the gravel road past the big curve about a hundred yards off, not looking good, too thin, carrying for a bag a battered paper sack. Jeff guesses his face's been scratched by briars in gullies where he's slept hitching back. From how far away? L.A., he answers, where Ray dumped him. In the kitchen, Jeff ladles beef soup into a big bowl and breaks bread he's just baked onto a plate. Go ahead. Take it, he says. Eat. He's happy he's back. On E.A.'s wrist is the broken band of the watch Jeff had given him. But nothing remains unsold to tick. E.A. takes it off and, returning what's left, with a string he uses to secure it, ties it round Jeff's thinner wrist, like a gold bracelet or chain he's won at a fair, having risked everything on one last throw of the ring.

The Killers

The No Vacancy Sign that shines outside
his window bleeds through the shut blinds.
On the unlocked door, on thin, useless
walls, bright lines hard as prison bars blink
on and off in time to the tick tock of a cheap
clock he keeps near a night stand to hear
how much slower it runs than his heart racing
to finish ahead of the rest of him lying
like an insomniac condemned to bed by a fatigue
too weary for sleep or death. He closes his eyes,
sees instead black sky and owl hungry night's
sharp beak keen for the heart of any nocturnal
creature scurrying like him over the forest's
floor from need or fear, the ravaging dark

circling over his head as calmly as if its prey
were already caught in its talons. Useless
to try to escape, useless to run, the night long
done with him before he was born. The stairs
outside his room creak until the pounding feet
sound like boots on iron or a cell slammed shut
by a guard, though there are too many shoes
marching down the hall to count how many
or to know whose foot kicks in the door, showing
off since they all know he knows it's useless
to latch it. "Fucking snitch," one screams, though he
was never told who he's supposed to have ratted
on. The boss wouldn't say, wouldn't give away
the name of the creep who preyed on him, still

a kid, still wet behind the ears, his brother said,
his tears innocent no matter what he did,
if anything. The boy's not surprised by the size
of the volley or by how many bullets pierce
his body before he dies. He never expected it
to end otherwise since the big boss never lies
about such serious affairs and like the law
he seems to be always refuses to intervene,
fate less stubborn than the gun in charge.
In the seedy bar downstairs, his killers drink
their whiskey straight and plug the jukebox full
of nickels. No thrills left, each returns to sleep
peacefully, his greedy hunger satisfied, his cruel
nature ratified for another day so easily by death.

Saipan

In her small sewing room--
her back erect, board straight,
imperial, her legs crossed
at her ankles, her hands

resting on the lace-covered
arms of her chair--Mother sits
waiting. Her fingers play with pins
that hold the doilies or twist tiny,

unraveling strands into knots.
With scissors from her basket,
she cuts them off, tugs the cloth
a fraction of an inch down

the chair's arm and re-pins it.
A high pitched cough starts
near the top of her lungs,
a hacking she is unable to stifle,

despite the hand she uses
to muffle the scary sound.

Advancing across Saipan's Tanapag
plains, my father was killed
by an enemy amputee
with a bayonet lashed to a pole

while parents shot, stabbed, and strangled
their children and threw them
over a precipice into the sea,
leaping in after them

even as General Saito
with a ceremonial sword drew
his own blood before an adjutant
shot him through the temple.

My father was one of thousands
who never came home.
Tangan-tangan like kudzu
has done its good work

to hide the unhealed
wounds and scars of war.

Once, in a childhood summer,
when I went for a swim
with my brother, I saw
how moonlight on his suit

made him shine like metal
or foil. Thirteen, he broke
his leg falling out of a tree
while he was cleaning leaves

off our roof after rain.
Stark naked, except for his cast,
he zipped from one end
of the hall on crutches as fast

as on his own two feet,
never needing to lean on me.

Our house's first floor is always
dark. Even under sun at noon,
shrubs block out the light.
In late spring or early summer,

devil's pincushions litter
the yard. Pfizer and creeping juniper
line our wall and walk.
Cerise and scarlet azalea,

forsythia, pink and white
indicas, pyracantha,
and rhododendron all compete
for air and light. Today,

the afternoon sun plays
on the leaves and needles
as on the surface of a pool,
seen from under water.

Not two days ago, I found
in the woods behind our house
a dog's corpse, ants crawling
out of its nostrils and over

its cloudy eyes, still open
as if alive to air and sky.

Mother's clothes are always
drab and musty, like the dark
brown bindings of the books
she inherited from her mother,

kept neatly shelved
and unread in her bedroom.
Now her whole body smells
discarded, as if it had lain

too long, slightly damp,
in a dim corner of the attic.

The night is obsidian, the moon
a white onion, slightly ovoid.
My brother sits for a while
on a park bench, a thing of silver

in the night, trying to picture
our father and failing. A black,
gummy caterpillar inches
over my lap. I flick it

with a finger across the den,
then hunt for it under the floor lamp.

Outside, an apple green
luna moth flutters over my head.
His friend's sport car's
top is down. Wearing

my floppy pajamas and robe,
I pick the paper late off the lawn.
My brother runs round me,
sleek in his shorts and t-shirt,

and eases into the bucket seat
of the Healey without opening
the door, a beautiful thing
into another beautiful thing

so beautifully slipping
that the tightly wound spool
of my love unravels like a wide
silk ribbon from its bobbin

and scoops and leaps and dances
giddily in the air.

Halfway down, Mother
is standing on a stair.
She holds on to the banister
with both hands, her knuckles

white as cartilage. Left unbuttoned,
her pink bathrobe covers
most of her pink nightgown.
A drop of blood trickles

down her chin and neck. Her skin
is milk glass, her hair gray down
caught in a web of black netting.
When she begins to cough again,

blood oozes out of her mouth
onto to the fist she brings to her lips.

Wearing a yellowing lime-colored
apron, her stockings rolled over
her ankles, an old woman sits
on a porch, staring out toward passing cars.

Her driveway is overgrown
with scattered patches of grass
and weeds. On the yard are discarded
cinderblocks, car parts, pot shards,

a bashed-in wash tub,
crumpled boxes. The picked carcass
of a tractor has been dumped
near the woods. The roof's trusses

sag. The bullfrog green pond
waits for the algae to take
over her world. My father was born
a half mile down this asphalt road.

Her boy's rusty hair is scraggly
from sweat. He doesn't squint
in the sun's glare, but leans
a thigh against a headlight

of his Chevy and folds his arms
across his naked chest.
His canvas shorts' laces droop
over his crotch. He digs

his right toe into the soil
and returns my stare
as if daring a camera
to snap him. His life belongs

to his body. He has his car.
He is arrogant, he is beautiful,
and he will not scare. So the wound
opens again. Light filters

through dark trees. A summer
wind blows through my heart.

A sharp light scuttles leaves
from trees like a thunderstorm.
Clouds hang still-born in the sky.
I rip vines off a picket fence

and toss the pile of twigs
I've gathered into a gully.
My skin itches. A bicycle bell
jingles. Its tires hum on the sidewalk.

Shaken leaves, rustling, release
a dead limb to topple to the earth,
splitting as it falls. The back screen
squeaks open. My brother stands

on the stoop. "It's Mother," he cries.
"I can't open her door."

After the war, Mother still hunted
with her father on a swamp ridge
near his home in Chowan on land
bordering the Chatanooka Cut

Indians once had roamed. One day,
they discovered among carvings
on an old overgrown tree
the portrait on an ancient beech

of her lost husband, cut into bark
a century before he was born.

Whether we attack or whether we stay,
there is only death. A Japanese officer
beheads his little band
of enlisted men with his sword

before he is shot down
by his would-be captor.
Japanese soldiers swim
to the reefs of Tanapag Harbor

where most are machine-gunned.
Natives leap from the cliffs
of Marpi Point to the knife-like
rocks below, the waters so clotted

with bobbing bodies that small craft
cannot steer a course without running
over them. Seven lives to repay
our country. Before he dies,

General Saito eats canned crab meat,
drinks sake. The lame, the halt,
the blind come forth from hospitals
to die. Charging toward a bayonet,

my father closes his eyes,
then mine in terror.

In our living room, my brother pushes
my legs where they rest to the back
of the couch to make space
and sits down, grabbing my hand.

I take his shoulder in my arms,
nudge him gently aside
and rise to walk toward the fireplace
where he follows me, no one left

in our house except us two
now, brothers, lovers,
eager unlike Mother to close
for good all our blinds and shades.

An oak tree scratches the top edge
of the picture window. Startled,
I look over his shoulder
and see in the dark

not my face reflected on the pane
but our father's, slightly smudged
and boneless like a saint's face
imprinted on a shroud I saw

in Spain whose rotting threads
no suppliant was allowed to touch.

The Road from Hessenberg

1945

A village, town under bombardment is worse than German woods for getting lost in. Mike kicks a burning door open for Les to lob a grenade through. A dud. Two women, suicides, lie in a bedroom corner, one slumped over the other, luger fallen beside a cat box, one face pressed into another like a child's against a mirror. Their mingled blood is staining a blue rug brown. On fire, lace curtains blacken into ashen threads that hover like gnats in the stifling air. Downstairs, the cellar stinks of rot. A dying German soldier's eyes are pale green, like baby leaves. After he quits breathing, Mike takes a leather shoemaker's apron off a hook to shield his face and chest from rats.

Night is falling, though the village streets are still bright from fire. Day's drizzle turns into rain and thunder. Masonry bits drip from the cellar's ceiling into a pool, scummy as a frog pond back home. Rain trickles through a dozen cracks. Nearby, a bomb bursts or a house blows up or a store of ammunition explodes. A loud whine follows, a child's shrill cry, a wail. When, curious, Les lifts off the leather shroud, the soldier's eyes have turned white as tallow rendered from a hog. Now and in the hour of our death, Mike says, his own flesh spotted with blood dried brown as the eyes on potato skin.

The rain turns to mist but the hot ruins still steam. In Thiessen, five miles east, a new shelling starts. Like silent waves, the fog rolls in and out of Hessenberg's streets, but settles in a church whose cracked bell lies in a pile of charred beams. Bits of stained glass, melted and remolded by fire, litter the sanctuary where Mike, Les, and Stu huddle to sleep for an hour or two.

At first light, they move forward, their boots clopping on cobblestones. First Mike, then Stu stumbles on rubble. Les trips on a root or taut rope. Glancing back, he glimpses a black hand and arm and a .38. Near woods, the fog disperses. A broken plow lies twisted behind a dead horse. Mangled train tracks run next to a river in which a bridge has sunk like a boat bow. Their roofs whole, their boxwood hedges neat, trim, thatched cottages line the road to a station platform. From one, Stu steals sausages he dangles round his neck. They eat them cold, though greasy as melting lard.

A half hour, an hour later, three kraut soldiers climb out of the river bed. They see Mike aim his rifle and freeze. Not men, but boys, their uniforms pickings from the dead. A blond kid stumbles forward. Piss stains his pants. He kneels on the grass and lays before him pictures he's been gripping in his fists, displaying them like a poker hand he's proud of, slowly, one at a time. Family photos. Treasured snapshots. Who knows. Rifle steady, Stu is still chewing some wurst gristle. The boy hugs his stomach from hunger.

Or fear. He knows where to look. Something bright, like sunlight reflected off a mirror or tin, shines from the railroad tower. The first shot hits another boy, poking his head over a hedgerow, sticking his hands up by the road. Blood gushes out of his chest. Stu and Les duck under boxwood while Mike tries to grab the blond kid to safety, out of the line of the sniper's fire. But, frightened, brawnier than he looks, the boy breaks free and runs for the orchard where a blast almost beheads him, like an ax too dull to make its cut clean. Another shot strikes Mike, who, screaming, grabs his thigh and knee. Recklessly, Les races to the platform and dashes through the tower's doors. Once lit, the station burns quick as a hay barn torched with kerosene.

From air, from ground, along every road, all Germany is burning down, town after town. Thank God, Les says to no one but a silent sky. He walks slowly back to Mike and tosses him a white skull and crossed bone patch flecked with gore. Thank God.

Long promised trucks and jeeps enter Hessenberg too late for much relief. Waiting for a medic, Les, as Stu had done, slows the blood seeping from Mike's shattered shin. He's being carried on a stretcher to a van headed west when Les and Stu ride off with a fresh division for Thiessen. Before they can reach the town, it's been pounded into stones, not a soul left alive to fight back. Rumors are flying through the troops that the Russians have advanced to Berlin's borders, that Hitler is dead, that Germany will surrender soon, at midnight tonight, tomorrow, or the next day at noon. Though no one can know if any are true, they faithfully believe them all.

In the foxholes in France, he and Mike would rub each other's feet. They still lost toenails. Replacements called them old. They fought their way together out of woods, down and up gorges, along icy roads. The sun shone when they crossed the Rhine into Germany. Mike tried to write twice a week to his wife Bea. But no pen would write in such cold. His last pencil was a stub. He'd run out of paper just before Hessenberg. Bad news, he'd said to Les. Bad luck. Still advancing, Les feels for the cross he wears round his neck along with his dog tags and taps the bronze cross bars.

As Les slogs through a beet field north of Thiessen, a light rain drizzles. Ahead of him, Stu is manning a flamethrower, destroying what's left of the crop in a storage bin a sniper had shot from. The farmer stands in a furrow and weeps. Les tugs on the strap of his canteen, half full of some kraut rot-gut brandy he poached from the farmhouse before this one. They tested it on a dog. No more poison than what had sickened him and Mike ages ago in a London pub. Never mind. The true adventure of a soul is to learn to stay home. Les stares up toward heaven. The planes are theirs. They own the skies.

1950

The proud courthouse soldier is shaded by an oak already old before Johnny Reb was cast in bronze fifty years before their war began. Les parks his truck in a slot outside the antique general store. Inside, Mike reads a ledger wide as his desk. Swiveling in his chair, he props his crutches against a crowded case displaying glass lamps and chimneys crowned by marble colored shades. Clutching a hankie, his wife helps a customer in front who leaves too quickly, the bell over the door tinkling again. Mike slides a drawer open, removes a jug, takes a big swig, offers Les some, sneaks it back into his desk.

A black man is stripping the basins, pails, hub caps from a wall and hooking hats and necklace beads to a plywood board alongside racks of ladies' dresses. With a pencil nub, Mike marks columns with minuses or zeroes. From his jacket, he takes a fresh deck, proposes poker. When the jug appears again, Les agrees to a quick game of gin but cannot lose a hand, no matter how hard he tries.

He should be home working on his farm. And might be if polio hadn't struck Mike's son Roy and killed him, only four years old. At the grave, Bea fainted. The preacher assured her that among all the wee ones who've died too young her boy was the spark flying closest to the Lord. He lit a match for her to see, but Bea blew it out.

When Mike bets five, Les shoves it back with the stack he's won even though he cheats not to win but to lose even more. No one's as unlucky as Mike. It's fate, he says, shrugging, God's will, and forces the bills into Les's jean's hip pocket. He means for me to get beat and you to keep it. It's like war. Kill or get killed. You reap what you sow. And so forth, Mike says with a grin he usually reserves for the girls who come in for a nickel's pack of gum or a cream soda.

Bea doesn't know what to do when her husband and Les go, leave the store open or lock it. No one ever buys what they sell anymore except for a cheap chew, cigarettes, penny candy, or a headache remedy, not enough for a livelihood for one, let alone two, or more again some day, God willing. Mike's good leg thumps down the wood walkway. Those boys. They'll drive to the river and fish off a tree stump all day as lazily as when they were kids. Not that she minds. Since her baby died, it's all she can do to keep busy.

1955

Les's truck passes what used to be Mike's store, now a chain Five and Dime. The old hospital's become a library. Where the town's lone boarding house stood is a new movie theater. Under its marquee a crowd huddles. A few dash for their cars parked along the sidewalk in front of the courthouse. During the storm, the clock dings each stroke like rain pinging on a roof.

Les lets his windshield wipers tick while he waits outside Mike's beaten down ivy-covered cottage. Gangrene. The key's in Les's pocket. Inside, the place smells like a churn. Bea's dress rustles, her slippers shuffle across the floor until he turns away. In the bedroom, a candle stub burns in a pewter holder on the seat of a stool. Les presses his ear against Mike's chest and closes his eyes, their lids dirty gray like old bone.

Fearful of doctors, Bea looks as scared as she sounded on the phone. She sits in a straight back chair and twists a button on her dress, gazing at the ceiling, its plaster cracked, discolored, dripping from the rain. She pleads with him. She needs a car, bus, or train ticket, some means of escape. Les offers his truck, the least he can do, and sets off on foot toward his farm, five miles off the new highway.

It's two o'clock in the morning. The muddy shoulder is tangled with weeds and vines. Like a trip wire, one catches his foot, toppling him into a sewage ditch. As he scrambles out, scratched and cut by briars, defiant, his fists pound the air.

The rain stops before dawn when the birds start to chatter. He wanders across a field and through woods to the river where, sitting on a boulder, he watches the water from the late storm overflow the banks. Grabbing a branch of a sycamore that had collapsed during the night, he climbs down its fallen moss covered trunk to where the branches sink. The sun glares through low clouds. Two crows cling to a pine limb and caw at squirrels shinnying up its trunk. Far off, nearer his farm, a hound brays at the last sliver of the moon. Les tosses a clay clod into the river to test its strength as it rushes west through thick brush banked by forest.

1960

Since Hessenberg, Bea knew she could never love Mike more than Les did. But she's grown too tired to fight their old battles anymore, remembering what they had said when groggy with beer, or to listen again in her head to Mike's story about how he'd failed to drag a boy safe from a sniper's bullet. He couldn't save his own son either or in his death spare Les. She hasn't budged from the swing all night. At first light, she unties the green velvet ribbons that bind her hair, already more gray than brown, and lets it down over her shoulders. The soft dawn colors her hands pale as the lace round her wrists or the old maid's collar on her dress.

She stares past the neighbor's shacks and cane toward the river far off. From a sweater pocket, she removes the picture she'd saved from a chest she'd been compelled to sell, the only photo she possessed of Mike, mailed to her from London shortly before he sailed for France. He's wearing his sergeant's stripes and his big grin, as he always did then. Les's standing beside him, his arm round his shoulder. Had either of them ever guessed how much more handsome both were when they stood next to each other?

Peach blossoms fall onto her hair and lap, but she shakes them off. A stray dog, maybe wild, rustles through bushes. She tries to shoo it away, but decides instead to treat it with the kibble she bought for her own ravenous hounds. As it laps up the bowl, she torches the snapshot with a stove flame and drops its ashes in the trash can under the sink. Too many years have passed. She will give no more nights to those she has lost, suffer no more nightmares of a boogyman God taking potshots at his children from a tower just to show off his power over innocents, like that boy in Hessenberg, like Roy. Like Mike. Like Les. Like her. The dog licks her hand, begging for more. She picks up the bowl. Wide is the road that leads to death, she sings, and thousands walk together there. She misses them all.

The House on Telegraph Hill

1.
At the foot of Telegraph Hill,
on every side except the western,
lies rubble--stones, large rocks,
small boulders the only enduring signs

of all that has plunged or slid
or been pushed off its cliffs
for generations after winter torrents.
In one story, a man was said

to have shoved his wife through a hole
in a shed floor that dangled
over a backyard edge.
The tale is tangled, woven

from old threads of false love
and greed made much knottier
on the screen by forgotten histories,
lost documents, and a boy's

considerable inheritance.
But listen closely to the Hill's
green parrots' chatter
as they eat their berries and nuts

and you may hear as others have
the earth's unease with its solid
self or the nearly mute cry
of a woman plummeting

from a high ledge of the house
she, not her husband owned.

2.
Wearing a gold-embroidered caftan,
holding a tonic by a hand
each of whose fingers is ringed
with jewels, he stands a bit shakily

in the driveway next to the boulevard
that curves in front of his mansion,
whose boxy façade conceals
the interior of a Venetian palazzo--

the boy he wittily calls his Leander
clad in snug swim trunks
and tight tank top,
ready for a swim across

the Hellespont, but bearing
the umbrella that protects Whitney
from the downpour as he chats
with Bill, his next door neighbor

who lives in the near collapse
of a one room earthquake cottage
where every day he types
his novels or the story of his life

in the CP, his assault on the Nazi flag
raised on the Bremen in New York's
harbor, the war he fought in Spain
with the Lincoln Brigade, in Germany

after, his old rifle, still good,
hanging on the wall over the table
he uses as a desk beside photographs
from newspapers of his comrades,

the three killed at Jarama River,
the four along the Rhine,
in pride of place: the two of them,
Bill and Whitney, lamenting

quietly to one another the months
of storms that have followed
too many years of drought,
Bill wearing his old war slicker,

the only one he owns,
as the water flows down
from Coit Tower over Whitney's slippers
and Bill's brogans, soaking them both,

though neither retreats into
his dry abode, too fascinated
by the hilltop lake to quit
surveying it yet, worrying

about more mud and rock
slides on the northeast side--
two houses having already
collapsed and fallen into

the rubble at the base--
wondering how safe the south slope
behind them is, the two of them
friends for that moment

who ten years before
would have had each other shot.

No More

The sky's overcast, dingy, mud gray. A north
wind blows, stark, rheumy, threatening snow.
Uptown, waiting for lights, people mass
near curbs against the cold. Wes wraps a scarf
round his neck, dons a suede bomber coat,
fleece lined gloves, shit kicker flier's boots–
a brother's remnants from the war he'd also
fought in. Block after block, his soles, heels clickclomp,
mocking his soldier's marching stride.
The museum's chilly as a marble vault. The boy
he's meeting stands next to a Bronzino, posing,
aping the sneer of the kid in the portrait, thinning
his lips, posturing to mimic his aristocratic,
disdainful power before he ghost-like vanishes

into the holy blacks, vermillions, prussian blues
of the Spanish renaissance. An hour later, when
Wes knows to find him there, he's waiting next
to the Met's outdoor pool. His glove's floating
toward the fountain's center. His right hand's
pink from the stinging wind. Dashing, brash,
he tugs off the other glove and tosses it in.
He grins at Wes, but doesn't talk as they ride
the subway, walk through the Village, their lapped
shadows gray as old snow, darkened by coal
soot or grime. Jack always leaves too soon.
Wes lies on a mattress he's shoved back to
the brighter of his rooms and snuggles beneath
the covers, tucking a blanket under his chin.

Snow cloaks the roofs, fire escapes, ledges of
the buildings across the alley. Aerials, poles,
slack wires forest the tenements. Carbolic,
sharp, an odor seeps through his floor. Black clouds
drift over head. The sky is hushed, moonless.
Their bodies had folded together like paper sheets
along the crease. He cannot sleep. Next morning,
he watches the ferries dock, commuters disembark,
pigeons swarming round their feet, unfrightened,
slow to rise in panicky flight. Workers
fit girders on the top floor of a new building
at Fiftieth and Park. Nearby, he drinks coffee,
eats strudel, strolling afterwards to check out
skaters or the oversized picture Christmas tree.

On fancy store windows, faces blur like a film
frame melting. Along Forty Second, he reads
new graffiti scrawled over the old, tries to
decipher the palimpsests on the stairwell's white
tiles, cryptic, violent, frantically drawn.
For fifty cents, he buys a triple bill he sleeps
through. Near the park, the night clear, wind
rattles tree limbs along the wall. Five hansoms
linger in line. The tang of horse flesh and piss
hangs in the air. Limousines and taxis wait
in front of the bustling hotels. Buses zoom
back and forth. A bum stumbles and thrusts
his bird claw hands under Wes's jaw. Weightless
as a ragged robe, his body sags on crutches.

His purple lips are swollen. Wes drops change
into his encrusted palms, but the beggar falls,
crashing flat, hard, on the sidewalk, cracking
bones. Wes calls for help. No one stops. Escaping,
he runs down stairs to the subway. In front of
his building, Wes hesitates, its façade menacing
and raw as the bum's scarred face. In his room,
he strips and lies on the floor. In reverie,
he touches Jack's sable hair, smells his skin,
tastes his tongue tasting his, their bodies
beating gently like leaves in a breeze. But
the beggar he'd left for dead stretches out
his arms to hold him instead, become a kebold,
gogmagog, or zombie who's snuck from his lair

into the city, like the kid on the subway ride
back, a tiger's face stitched on his shiny jacket,
who slashed at a soldier leaning on a cane,
lovers on a bench, a woman wearing a smart
gray dress and a Santa cap, and Wes--jabbing
at all five with his knife, long, broad, sharp
as a bayonet. A knock on his door breaks what
spell he's in. It's Jack, battered, clothes torn
again. He coughs, swears, licks blood off his lips.
His body shakes, buzzes like a fly's as it dies,
as Guy's did, too, in Tinian that time. And Joe's.
Those who beat him do a swell job. Jack passes
out. As he rests, his smile's sly as a Buddha's.
He sleeps till dawn slides back through buildings.

Sleet's falling intermittently. Wes opens a cedar
chest, throws Jack another blanket, sweet
with resin and a hint of camphor. He draws it up
to his chin, stares at a bulbless socket, his face
as sad as an actor's peering through the curtain
at an empty house. Wes contemplates a patch
of plaster, cracked and crumbling. No more dark,
Jack. No more wars. No more torture. Let them
tan on a beach instead as seabirds clatter, tides
lap pebbles along the shore. Let them walk
down stairs carved from rock, the cliff behind
them starry from quartz. In a shower, let steam
mist the room, metal doors slam, shoes shuffle
as they shut off their faucets at the same time

and, reaching for the same towel, touch. Let him
taste the wax in Jack's ears, kiss his fingernails'
moons, lips, zipper scar on his butt. Let the sun
always shine. Let all this mourning stop. No
more will he look for Jack past machine shops,
trucks, and piers to where men's faces leer out
of the dark, guarding the way to an open yard
fenced in by corrugated tin and sheet metal,
requiring a pass word to enter, and walk
a ramp past a bebop blast and the stench of grease
sweat, beer, urine, leather, jizz to a black ring
of men hunched over, drunkenly cheering, buzzing,
yelling, swearing like betters huddled round
a cock pit or crap game, whips stinging his flesh

while guards behind Jack hold torches like monks
ready to set fire to the faggots they've piled beneath.
No more will he see shadows fall across his body
as Jack smiles, his eyes too proud not to mock
a pain only more pain will save him from. No more.
He can't watch anymore. This war's over. Outside,
clouds absorb the sky's ink like cotton. Wes draws
Jack's jacket's collar higher, his shirt sticky
from blood. His sudden desire scares him like
a dud grenade. In a brownstone, his shades still up,
a hunk strips as the moon slips behind a taller
building, flattening it like a fence picket over
which a shadow arcs, a black rainbow that leads
Wes's anxious eye from one night to another.

Say I Have a Son

Say I have a son. (I have always wanted
a son.) Say just after he turns five he starts
to fear the dark. To hear his muffled cries,
I keep our doors open wide. Three or four
times a night, he wakes me, my wife. If I
read to him he grows tired, quiet. Set back
down in his bed, he falls quickly asleep.
But soon a new terror begins. I must hold him
longer. I must comfort him more. Say a doctor
insists we not coddle him. Say my wife begs
me to stop. She can bear it no longer.
I close my boy's door. I shut my own. His cries
are useless as prayers. No light will shine
again for him. Yet still he stares into the night.

Say he fights through France in woods, blasted
trunks, shattered limbs. As each tree is hit,
he shoots the rats that gnaw their roots raw.
At dawn, he fires at snipers. A mine blows off
a kraut's arm. I have heard, as a train breaks,
its wheels shriek on track. So he shrieks.
So, too, does my son, a crater yawning yards
away in which one of his soldier's been torn
from his grave, his bones bark dark, his clothes
peeling off his flesh like sunburned skin.
Nothing is what my son says. Nothing. The best
lookout by day, the sharpest at night. No fighting,
no artillery, no enemy moving either way.
Just nothing, nothing, nothing to see, my son.

Say in forty-six they fly his body back home
to his wife who lives far away in the delta.
I hire a car. Her younger brother drowned
in Leyte. She and her mother live alone.
She tidies the house most days. For three years
it's never quit raining. We stand at the foot
of his makeshift plot. I lean against a wall
pocked with broken roses from stained glass
shards. A searing heat blows across the yard,
a bayou swelter that's news to me. My boy's
grave's dirt's blacker than the river silt
she skims to nourish her wilting garden. Say
he sleeps peacefully now, my son, unafraid,
lights off, behind a door I hated to close.

Nietzsche in Manhattan

Apollo, Dionysos: strict law and raucous
joy, temple and bacchanalia, a glacier,
crystal perfect, melting into ocean,
molten lava cooling into rock. His mind,
his cock. Life's a rigid king beset by
maddened women, reason by ecstasy.
Coal and flame, cobalt and purple
petals, iron's rust, gold's dust–natural
hues he could have used more. Think of
a statue twined with vine, like linen, unrolled
though still unsized, stapled to stretchers.
So, too, his studio's silent as heaven.
Close the door, the windows, turn off
the light. Play the game. Loose the mob.

His pictures straddle walls. His palette knife's
too dull, but the blade he uses to slice linen's
sharp. The pain is worse than he'd feared.
His veins drip cadmium light on the floor,
viscous like the quick drying oils he loathed.
Not slumping, he sits up proudly in his chair,
his bloody left hand clutching the blade
that sheers what it seeks, the second slice
quicker, more final. He's scripted his last words
as if his death were a play no one knows
to attend. Sweetest blade, he whispers self-
mockingly, my Apollo. Dearest blood, my
Dionysos. Now enemies, now unwise lovers,
always brothers: my life, my eyes, my many colors.

As I Live and Breathe

Working in her garden, his mother wears
manly shoes, rolled up jeans, a checkered
shirt, an embroidered vest, cloth gloves
with rubber palms and fingers. A blue bandana
grips her red hair as she prunes, nurses
her thinning roses. Behind her, black columns
of hickory, pine, tulip poplars, and oak
soar and arch high as church windows. Her son
sits on the stone wall of a bridge. A year
before, he saw his brother killed in Kwajalein.
Leaves bristle in the breeze. Before an August
thunderstorm, the rhododendron and laurel
tangled together smell burned, like dusty,
metallic air along a tank track after battle.

A man's belly button, shiny and pink, the tufts
of hair below, the thighs, the knees, skin
the color of burned butter, china doll eyes
set in a tough guy's head. Dreams. Outside,
a truck sputters and stalls. With the back of
his hand, he wipes sweat beads off his brow.
Across the road, an old friend cries, "As I
live and breathe, I thought you were dead."
It's no surprise. He's seen his twin, too,
a rifle strapped to his back, turning a corner,
chomping on the stogie he'd learned to smoke
in the army, a scruffy mutt tugging on its leash
as a sharp orange light pierces the morning
mist that peaceably steams off the macadam.

His father sits in his white oak chair in
front of the choir. His right foot rises, falls
in a slow, dazed tapping. His electric blue
jacket hangs off his shoulders. Two deacons
open the rattling church windows. Winds flip
the bible's pages as his father gapes out
at thunderheads, grackle black and iridescent.
By the cemetery grow datura, columbine, salvia,
phlox, and honeysuckle crusted with nectar,
yellow like cut corn or mown hay or flakes
of a moth's golden wings he'd spied that dawn
dangling from a perfect spiderweb as tautly
threaded through bush twigs as a cat's cradle
between the fingers of his brother's deft hands.

Pilgrimage

1.
Like crushed oil on asphalt,
red, gold, and blue rings
halo the moon. Three days
ago, his mother slumped

in her chair, dead, clutching
a hand to her bosom, her glasses
crooked on her nose. Moths
whirl round his porch light

like bees about a hive or swarm
over head. Slug slime trails
across the steps. He crushes
a black beetle inching up

the screen and flicks the mashed
carcass into a shrub. A breeze
rattles spindly dogwood branches.
Gardenia and japonica tickle

his nose. The Clarks' big Rott
barks at a cat or bats swooping
through the oak in their backyard.
Dash jumps the gulch that borders

the woods he crosses to the long
abandoned pasture and the kid's
mini football field where milkweed,
sumac, and golden rod grow

hay high. Burrs sticking
to his slacks prick his skin.
Patches of wet sod smell
like clay clods the gravediggers

dug from his mother's plot.
A pickup brakes near a curve
in the road. Still moving too fast,
swerving, it skids past the goal post.

He hears in the tires' squeals
his brother's heaving into a bowl,
soaking the rug blood red.
Along sidelines marked

by stones and sticks, he races
to score an unassisted touchdown
in the dark. His young brother,
his mother cheer him on.

2.
Their daughters shooed off
to school, her kerchief tied
round her head, her blouse
tucked into faded jeans,

her hands protected by
Dash's leather work gloves,
Jennie waters her rows
of red and yellow tulips

blooming in front of a just pruned
backdrop of pink and white
azalea. With a hoe, she chops
the soil or knocks earth off

weeds' roots before she tosses
them into an old sheet
to haul them later to the mulch pile.
Pausing, she looks at Dash

and wipes a glove across
her sweating brow, dirtying
the deep furrows of her frown.
Perched on a bobbing stem,

a purple finch clamps its beak
on a fat berry. Two cardinals,
their feathers bright from a morning
shower, squabble in the hickory.

3.
His father sits on a stool,
a ripped cap on his head,
his skin cracked and sandy yellow
like chicken claws he claims to eat.

Drool dribbles off his chin
onto his weasel neck
and undershirt. With a finger,
he stirs the soggy cereal

he won't eat into mush. He needs
to blow his nose. He closes
his eyes. As tears trickle
down his cheeks, Dash walks

his father outside to sit under
a cherry tree where he can watch
birds hop and peck the ground.
He wipes under his eyes

and snotty nose with a towel.
The tree's flowers drop
like seeds into Penn's lap.
His fingers play with the petals.

He whiffs them, smiles, sniffs
again. Inside his parents' house,
Dash confronts the clutter:
cane chair, wicker rocker,

pine hutch, cupboards,
knickknack stand, cedar chest,
two green wine bottle lamps,
all built by his father, that Dash

has shoved into one small room
for a move Penn swears
he'll fight harder than he fought
the Japs he hated and hates still.

He's wheezing worse than one
of his lame asthmatic hounds
and shaking from a fit as Dash
lifts him into his house.

A clock chimes six.
Sunlight seeps through the bottles
Elizabeth found and placed
on their bedroom's window sill,

their colors blazing on the opposite wall
like stained glass in a church.
At work, Dash knows, old Walt's
locked the door after the Burtons

quit early for home, the tires
he told them twice to install
on a rush order still waiting
on the rack for his return.

4.
Green was his mother's color,
especially lime green or grape
or avocado. But her walls,
the chintz pillows, curtains,

tiny bed decorations long ago
faded to the chalky froth
of the lime sherbet and ginger ale
punch served at Dash's wedding.

Elizabeth's favorite photographs
sit on a swatch of apple green
lace on an oak dresser.
Her daughter's pose shows off

the perfect line of her nose
and neck and fine cheekbones.
She chose Dash's army picture
because he'd smiled for once.

But she showed Tim's photo
in the middle, pride of place.
He'd taped a peace symbol
on his mortar board, his long blond hair

whipping in the wind, two fingers
forming a V, the only Penry
to graduate from college.
Not gay, but a pilgrim, he told her

that night, to which Elizabeth replied,
A pilgrim, dear? Then you must go,
do whatever you need to do,
while blessings pour on you every day.

5.
Jennie's still awake,
a seed and garden magazine
open on her lap. Worry stiffens
her face. As he crosses the porch,

Dash looks beyond the screen,
up into the dark as if he's searching
for the star assigned to him at birth,
dim and small and far away.

His wife closes her magazine
and drops it to the floor,
breathing in deeply, relishing
her roses. He drifts toward her,

his nerves dull, his muscles
useless, like when he was caught
in rapids he could not fight
but had to ride all the way.

The wicker chair creaks
as she stands up. He moves
to touch her cheek or hair,
but she recoils, backs out of reach,

and passes through the door
into the long black hall
beyond their daughters' rooms
to hers, alone. He turns to listen

to the locusts droning, even louder
after a shower, and to smell
the sticky honeysuckle,
both like grass dizzying his brain,

confusing his senses. He abandons
the porch and circles the pine grove
to his car in the driveway.
A need to sob pierces his gut,

but he tightens his muscles
and grabs an oak branch
to steady himself, the frogs' croaking
also heady in his ears. As he drives off,

trees webbed with caterpillar tents
and wild rose thickets
blooming roadside shine
in his headlights. Last summer,

able to stand only by gripping
the back of a chair, staring
out the window of Dash's bedroom,
Tim swore the tangled profusion

of Jennie's flowers and all
the wild woods beyond their yard
were in their fine excess
the true face of God

that only sex had revealed
to him so clearly before,
neither smiling nor frowning,
but always beckoning him to more.

6.
Thunder rumbles across the sky.
Whatever the weather tomorrow,
Dash will work on Penn's barn.
That job done, he'll paint the roof

and shingles and repair the wiring
in the house. He'll replant
some of the fields, left fallow
far too long. He'll need

to keep busy, ready to sell
when it's time. Soon Dash
will have to find his father
wherever he's wandered off,

inside or outside the house,
unlace his boots, his socks
reeking, and carry him to bed.
As Penn lies on his mattress,

its springs will sag and he'll glare
at the light fixture on the ceiling
filled with insect carcasses
and bitch again about the sores

on his legs as Dash unfastens
his pants and tugs them off.
He'll struggle with his teeth
and set them next to the old

army pistol Penn swears
he'll shoot himself with,
using bullets he's concealed
God knows where. Dash

doubts he'll ever find them,
however hard he looks,
not even if he stares straight
into his father's eyes,

as if the solution to his secret
hides behind them, like clues
to the world at his birth
no father ever tells his son.

The Birds

Only on the obscurest nights do ravens
dance by owlight to all who care to watch
invisible in the dark. And as they perform
their homage to balletically graceful birds,
like the hummingbird stilled by its beating wings
or a hawk in spiraling flight, they sing in a clacking
voice of all the grace they lack. Those croaking
songs are all of their dance you're likely to see
as these blackest invisible birds prance at
midnight in May when like every creature every
soldier lying dead in his restless bed spies
through the lies of a raven's song the truth
of the raven's dance: the past's an art of
unseen wings that beat in the visible dark.

Acknowledgements

I am deeply grateful to the poets Linda Gregg and Bill Mayer for their introductions to this book.

I offer my thanks, too, to Steve Arkin, Jo Keroes, Kurt Wilde, Jon O'Bergh, Diane Strommer, Elizabeth Spinner, and, in particular, Robert Mohr, as well as many other friends, for patiently reading these poems in their various versions over the year of the book's evolution.

Some of these poems, a few in different versions, have previously appeared in literary magazines: The Ampersand, Danse Macabre, Five Fingers, Fourteen Hills, Prick of the Spindle, Vitruvius Journal, and The Write Room. My thanks go to the editors.

I'm indebted to the National Archives and Records Administration for the use of photographs from both the battlefields and home front during World War Two.

I owe to Gerald Coble, a friend and inspiration for over fifty years, much of the meaning and sense of my life. Once more his art enfolds my words. Thanks.
And thanks to Nathan Wirth for the author's photograph he kindly took one fine misty morning by the Pacific.

This book would not exist without the time, commitment, imagination, and labor its editor Robert Colley has given it. "All I want is a generous spirit in customs," Ezra Pound wrote late in life. That spirit informs Bob's work. It has been a great gift to me.

And to Atticus Carr my thanks for the love that sustains my life.